Release

Renee Breakthrough

Copyright © 2019 Renee Breakthrough
All rights reserved
First Edition

PAGE PUBLISHING, INC.
New York, NY

First originally published by Page Publishing, Inc. 2019

ISBN 978-1-64298-447-7 (Paperback)
ISBN 978-1-64298-448-4 (Digital)

Printed in the United States of America

> I have learned to accept the things that I cannot change and to change the things that I can. I live by the Serenity Prayer. What is God's ultimate purpose for our lives?

I WAS BORN IN 1961 ON the southwest side of Detroit. My father was a military man, and my mother was a young housewife with five children. I remember growing up with lots of love. Although we were poor, the love my parents and grandparents showed us made us feel privileged. I remember my mother and father being loving and teaching us how to have respect for one another. She had her first child born at the age of fifteen, and then me 10 months later. I have two sisters and two brothers. My oldest sister was always overprotective of our family. Although I'm the second oldest of five, my grandmother used to say that I have an old soul like I've been here before. I never had the time to go outside and play with my friends. I always was responsible for taking care of my younger siblings.

My father's parents were professional working people. My grandfather worked at a steel mill, and my grandmother was a nurse at the time. My grandfather being the only child, they were very wealthy. His parents owned a funeral home, and acres of pecan trees. They had a total of nine children together. My mother's parents were very loving and caring toward us. My mother's mother also, had eleven children of her own. My mother's father was also a military man like my dad. My grandfather served in World War II, and received the Parachutists' Badge, American Theater Ribbon, and the Victory Medal. He had two children six months apart; he decided to marry the woman who gave birth to his first male child. My grandfather and grandmother shared join custody of my mom. His wife even loved my mom just like she was her own daughter, she even had her own Strawberry Shortcake room. My grandfather told me it was the biggest mistake he had ever made. He should've followed his heart. My grandmother was the one he really loved. After he retired from the military, he worked at Ford Motor Company, his brothers and himself owned the whole block of Schafer. This included gas stations, liquor stores, and Chad's Rental Hall, etc. This is where my love for money came from. I remember my grandfather sitting me on his lap telling me about his military life, and adventures. My grandfather's and I shared a special bond, and people would say we look like twins. I would always stop by and see him, with his favorite ice cream. I loved to see his smile.

My mother and grandfather had a loving and respectful relationship until she got pregnant at the age of fifteen and married my father whom he disapproved of. My mother very first time being intimate with my father she became pregnant. Their relationship took a turn because of her choices, but it never changed the love he had for her. He started being less supportive financially because she was married to my father.

My mom and dad would always fight. My mom was tired of my father sending different women to her home, although he would receive money from them and hand it over to my mom. My dad was a man of many things. One of the things was pimping women, and he did not play when it came to his money. Although he never slept with them, it was just business; my mom wasn't having it. The money was adding to our income and paid the bills. We were living with my father's parents in Ecorse. While my father was in the military, me being five at the time. My father came home with some good news; he got approved for the land, to get our home build in Pontiac, Michigan. I remember my mother being so happy that she would have her own home built the way she wanted. This is where my princess story began. My sisters and I had our own bedroom. I thought we were the richest kids in the world. Always coming home surprising us, one day he surprised us with a cocaine-white blue-eyed

RELEASE

German shepherd named Bobo. Bobo was a very smart dog. He protected us when my dad was in the military.

My mother's personality was very loving, caring, sharing, and strong. I can remember sleeping with her when my dad was gone. My mother talking to me all night like I was an adult. How marrying someone in the military and missing them became hard at times.

At an early age, my mom started showing and teaching me how to grow into a responsible young lady. Two of my main responsibilities were showing me how to pay bills and make sure that I took care of my brothers and sisters. My mother always said life is short, and I don't know how long I'll be here, so I must teach you these things. At the time, I was only seven years old. Somehow, I was able to have a clear understanding of it all. She had my ear, she would consistently tell me how she believed I've been here on this earth before. My mother was fifteen when she had her first child. She would look at me and say everything that she is telling me today I would one day need in life.

I was a student at the time, on the honor roll by the age of seven. My mother and father were going through a lot of marital problems. The temporary separation, cause us to go back and forth to my mother's mom house. I just wanted to stay home, in my own room where everything was in order. One day my mom told me to go the store, which was on the corner from us, to get bologna and a few cans of tomato soup, what we called a "poor girl's lunch". Busy running from a mentally challenged boy who loved chasing me and throwing rocks at me, and he would always tell me I was going to be his girlfriend. After being chased I proceed to the store to get what my mother needed. I took so long at the store. By now my mother is looking for me. She was highly upset that I took longer than usual; she was more worried than anything. As I crossed the street to get closer to her, she was screaming my name through the window. Somehow the window broke and came down in pieces and mistakenly cut me across my face, near my temple and my left leg. My mom panicked and called the ambulance. I just remember waking up in the hospital with my mother and father arguing about what happened and him accusing her of not taking care of her kids. I wanted to get up and see my face, but my mother said, "Don't look in the mirror just yet, it may scare you because of the swelling." The doctor stated due to my injuries on my head it could later lead to autism because of the glass missing my temple by a hair. The side effects would be headaches, and a hard time with comprehension. Our faith was bigger than that thank God I was still alive. On the other hand, my father was furious. Making it plain that he still will hold me accountable for my actions, and not to use my injuries as weakness and let it hinder me.

My father was the disciplinarian, my siblings and I was afraid of him, but in a respectful way. We would get in trouble for the smallest things, like putting our hand prints on his car windows. He was a neat freak; always known for having an immaculate car. Like his father they had to have a brand-new car every two years. Both were ladies men. I thank God for how beautiful my mother was inside and out; they would say her five wonderful children look just like her, and the structure, and cleanliness from dad. Hanging out at Twenty Grand with her sister bragging how Smokey Robinson was all over her. That's when my aunt was dating David Ruffin from the Temptations. I thought they were overexaggerating about the whole situation until one day David Ruffin's chauffeur pulled up and David got out of it. I was outdone, amazing to see being a kid and all. I heard that Smokey Robinson was all in for my mother. I asked myself why would she stay with my father; he was very disrespectful and abusive. She could've had any man that would've treated her better. Her beauty shined so bright; She would always make excuses for why she did not want to leave. She loved him for being her husband and the father of her kids. She loved him 'cause she was a virgin to him. As history repeats itself the first time he touched her she became pregnant. She would always think about the one rule back in her days. No leaving your husband or children by any means.

I remember her crying herself to sleep every night missing my father because she loved him. We moved into a family flat above my grandmother (mother's mom). My mother began to date and see this guy. He wasn't attractive but was very nice, so we thought. My mother met him through my aunt, who was dating his brother at the time. My mother used to tell me that she didn't love him. She wanted to get my father's attention and show him how it feels to have a taste of his own medicine. They both were very miserable apart. My father questioned us when he came around about our mother's new guy friend. Asking us questions like "Does he touch us or disrespect us in any way?" He would say, "No matter who your mom deals with, they will never be your father. I am your father. This is temporary, I'll be back soon."

My father would be very disrespectful towards my mother's friend every time he was around. My father always carried a pistol and had one of his friends with him. My father would send his friend over to check on my mother every day and report back to him. He told us that something wasn't quite right about my mother's friend, he insisted that we be cautious and he would keep a close eye out. Sure enough, he was right. When I turned eight my mother's boyfriend moved in, then at night I started to have crazy nightmares that I was being fondled by someone; it was crazy. After my nightmares I would be scared to sleep at night.

I started spending weekends with my father's mother. I told her about those nightmares the same night. I begin to explain to her, I feel like someone is touching me between my legs with their fingers. My father mom didn't trust my mother's boyfriend, she felt his strange behavior. She stated to me that she was praying that my father get his act together because she knows he really loves my mother. "I love my family," and "I want them together. She said; "The next time you having those nightmares again, and it feel like someone is touching you; apply pressure to their fingers by bending them back and hollering for help. She needed to know before she had to use her pistol and kill him before her son do and go to jail.

My father was in the military at this time. My father's dad was being released from prison in a month. So we were getting ready to have a big "welcome home" party for my father's dad.

My Father's mom was getting ready to have surgery, and out of love and concern asking what's going on.

She said, "All, be quiet and don't start crying, it's a minor procedure. I should be home in a couple days."

RELEASE

My father's mom passing time was teaching us how to cook from scratch and teaching us how to carry ourselves with respect. We also learned how to make homemade ice cream from scratch. Be careful of whom you give your love to. "Love is power," she would always say. She had one friend that lived two houses down; he suffered from Autism. He was employed at Chrysler, when the time came he was able to get some of my family members a job. She treated him like he was her own brother. She was very loving, and if she bought for one, she bought for all her children and grandchildren as well.

On the way taking us home one night, she ask was I still having those crazy nightmares. She asked me to please not tell my father when he called. He would be worried he didn't like my mother's friend, and, he really didn't trust him around his family. She said, "I really need you to start paying attention to your surroundings, because your mother is starting to act strange. My mom and her boyfriend were locking themselves in the bathroom. I believed they were getting high. My grandmother told me to watch them, and I started being suspicious and keeping a close eye. She started not to pay us any attention like she used to; she was drifting away and always in a daze.

One night I was asleep, and I started having one of those crazy nightmares again. I did just what my grandmother told me to do holding on to his finger, screaming and hollering. He quickly put his hand over my mouth to get me to stop screaming. I was still holding his fingers, bending them backward and forward. I was saying to him, "Do you know if I tell my father what you just did to me", He going to kill you! He stated he was sorry; "Please don't tell nobody," and he would not do it again. He loved my mother very much, he thought she was pregnant. I stopped bending his fingers and ran in the room where my mother was.

I was just shaking her out of her sleep, saying, "You're pregnant, you already have five children. Why? Have more by a man other than my father." She woke and yelled, "No, I'm not pregnant, I'm just worried about your grandmother's surgery tomorrow." She told me to lie back down. "Everything will be okay." Horrifying to know all the time when I had these crazy nightmares, they were real.

RELEASE

I always thought I was the protector of my mom, so I held back my secret to protect my parents, family, and grandparents, 'cause I knew they would have killed him. I fell asleep in my mother's arms. Waking up the next day, with my mother getting us ready for school. While preparing to go to the hospital with my dad for my father's mother surgery. I can remember that June morning we prayed for my grandmother. Something just wasn't feeling right all day at school. I was so excited when school let out, so I could check on her. Arriving home I noticed a lot of family members at the house. Everyone in the house was screaming and crying, my father and grandfather said to us, "Your grandmother has passed away." I just remember looking at my sister. My grandmother and her were really close. I ran to my sister and held her as we shed tears, saying, "I don't believe it!" I never had a chance to tell her my nightmares were real! Looking at my father, I knew I could never share with him that my mother's boyfriend had been touching me. Which would have devastated him at this moment, especially after losing his mother. Wow, so much to take in for one day. My grandfather told my father he's the oldest and gave him the responsibility of making funeral arrangements for my grandmother. That night I remember crying myself to sleep, waking up to my mother's boyfriend's voice whispering in my ear. "I'll never touch you again. Please don't tell your father or anyone else. I'm going to get some counseling."

    I know my father would have killed him and anyone that touched us. I decided it wasn't the right time to tell my father. His siblings were already fighting over the arrangement of my grandmother's funeral and the money she left behind. It was a very sad time for us. It just seemed unbelievable that she left us. I found myself very upset with God. How could this happen. She was a churchgoing woman who believes in God. She kept us all in church three times a week.

    My mother woke us up, to get ready for the funeral. I was dressed, sitting in the window, waiting for the funeral cars to come. Once they arrived, two men got out of the cars, looking like something out of a horror movie. But the guys were very nice and polite. They opened the doors for us and drove us to the church where they had my grandmother. It was crazy, I had been in this church so many times, now I was scared to go in and see my grandmother lying there lifeless. My father grabbed me and my sister's hand and walked us up to the casket, making us kiss my grandmother goodbye. I was crying and screaming; I didn't want to kiss her. My grandfather immediately picked me up and put me on his lap and said, "You can't be afraid of the dead, it's just her shell. She is in heaven looking down on us smiling now." I just didn't want to hear that. I told my grandfather I never had a chance to tell her something, and he said, "You can tell her, she hears you." I looked around the room; everybody was in tears. What a sad day.

The funeral service was almost over, and they are getting ready to close the casket. My father's baby sister started screaming and having a fit. She was mourning and crying out for her mother. I remember my father going over to console her; it was a moment I'll never forget. We were leaving church and heading to the cemetery. I was thinking she cannot breathe in that box; how could God allow this to happen? We needed our grandmother. She was the only one to keep our family together, now my family was falling apart.

Got back home that night, the child molester (my mother's boyfriend) was there. All I could do was run to my room and cry. My mother followed me with no idea what was going on. She thought I was crying over the loss of my grandmother still. I was scared to go to sleep. Thinking that he would to come into my room and touch me again. I know my mother would have killed him if she knew what he was doing to me. She was very protective over her kids, same as my father. My mother's boyfriend never touched me again. In fact, he stayed away from me.

My father had just lost one of his Army buddies. It was one of his close friends. In the process of consoling his friend's wife, they started dating each other. She had a disabled little girl. I know my father was a hustler and money chaser so he kept his best friend wife very close. He knew about her military death benefits, and what she was getting ready to receive from the government. He became very heartless, he was constantly getting into with his siblings, over my grandmother's possessions. One day my grandmother's coin collection came up missing. Rare coins my grandmother said she was going to give to us one day, a trunk full. My father's brothers and sisters accused him of taking all the coins. He wasn't taking care of us anymore; we had no support from him at all, and he lost our home in Pontiac. I overheard my father tell my mother that he made a few bad business deals. He missed his family, and he wanted to come home and be a family again. Charming my mother back in his arms. He knew how much my mother loved him. The other woman was in love with my father too! She wanted him to divorce my mother so they could be a family. My father said he was never going to move in with the other woman. He just wanted to make my mother jealous because she had another man sleeping with her sometimes. My father start spending the night over and spending more time with us.

Lying on the sofa one night with my sisters and brothers watching TV, we fell asleep. I was awakened by a man kissing me on my forehead. I was thinking I was having crazy nightmares again, to my surprise it was my father. Picking me up and putting me, my sisters and brothers in bed. "Things are about to change. I'm going to get my family back. I'm taking y'all to school in the morning; I miss y'all. We can talk and catch up on things."

So that next morning, my sister and I were walking to school with my father. We started to tell him what was going on. It was a big change from what we were used to. Losing the home in Pontiac and moving. We had to adjust to roaches, mice, and rats. It stank out here in Delray like dead dogs from the soap factory.

"Dad, you remember telling us not to eat over at my grandmother's house because she had roaches and mice? Saying they carry diseases and can crawl in your ears and lay their eggs. How can you allow us to live in those types of conditions now?" He said, "I know my mother would be very unhappy with me. I can't lose my family. I need your mother now, I want my life back." He said he would be back to pick us up after school and take us over to my deceased grandmother's house to meet my grandfather's new girlfriend. My sister and I told my father we didn't want to go; his new wife moved her whole family into my grandma's house.

My dad said, "It is what it is, life goes on.

RELEASE

I was very upset thinking that my grandma's body wasn't even cold yet and we already have a new grandmother. Nobody is going to take my Grandmothers place, and I was named after her. My father told us our aunt, which was his baby sister, would be moving in with us; she was his heart. He always looked for her whenever he comes over my grandmother house. We met my grandfather's new wife and her kids. They were very nice people; my grandfather seemed to be happy. I love him so.

Weeks went by, and my father was still at home with us. He was on a grieving pass from the Army. I overheard my father telling my mother that he was going to get out of the Army with an honorable discharge. I was so happy to hear that he was getting out. Once she decided to go back to my father, she realized she was pregnant. It was a strong possibility that it was her boyfriend's. My father being the only love of her life, her kids father. He was selfish and arrogant he would not allow another man's kid in his house. I believed that my mother decided to have an abortion, because she didn't know if my father was the dad. One morning, we were doing our normal routine getting ready for school. My mother was very happy and cheerful in a loving way. She said she would see us when we get out of school. My father picked us up from school telling me and my older sister to take care of our brothers and sister. "Your mother is not feeling her best, she has to stay downstairs with your grandmother." I asked why. He said, "Don't ask me nothing, just do what you are told. Watch after your sisters and brothers until your mom feels better." Pulling up at the house, we jumped out of the car to see my mother. I got in the house; she was lying in the bed looking very pale. She was just hugging and kissing me and my sister, telling us to watch over our siblings, because she wasn't feeling well. Shortly after she calls me and says, "Come here, whatever happens, promise me one thing you will take care of your siblings for me. I said, "Ma, why are you talking like that? I'm only nine years old." She said, "I need your ear, listen to me. Don't let nobody separate y'all." She repeated herself over and over again. "No matter what". I told her I was going to get my brothers and sisters then I would come back and lie down with her and hold her until she felt better. When I got upstairs, my older

RELEASE

sister had already got them together. She fed them and gave them a bath. I hurried up and ate and ran back downstairs to lie down with my mother so I can hold and comfort her until she fell asleep. I fell asleep as well until my sister came to wake me up, telling me I had to go upstairs. When I got upstairs a short time after, I heard sirens outside. I went over and sat on the stairs and watched them wheel my mother out on a stretcher. I went upstairs to tell my sister what just happened to our mother. They took her in the ambulance. We prayed and fell asleep holding each other.

A few hours later my aunt came in and upstairs to get me and my siblings; we went downstairs to hear the worst news ever in our lives. Our mother was gone and never coming back. Being just nine years old, I didn't understand death. But hearing that my mother was never coming back had me traumatized. Everyone was taking it bad; I excused myself and went upstairs to my mother's bedroom, got in her bed, and cried myself to sleep. Waking up the next morning, realizing that this wasn't a dream and my mother was really gone.

My father came that next day, explain what death was in his firm and blunt way. Reminding us he just lost his mother. I felt numb. How can this happen to my family? Who is going to take care of us? My dad wasn't in any shape to take care of us solely; he was getting high at the time. He got a new girlfriend, and my mother's mother had ten children; she was very poor had so little. She was already having a hard time; how could she take on five more children.

My mother's father had started drinking heavily, crying over my mother's death. She was his only baby girl. He never liked my father at all; they started arguing on who was going to pay for my mother's funeral. My grandfather knew that my father had a military insurance policy on my mother that doubled because her death was accidental. My grandfather new girlfriend convince him to bury his daughter. She and my mother had a great relationship; we used to spend nights over at her house. I enjoyed spending quality time with her and her family. She and my grandfather sent my mother to heaven like a princess. They had her in a gold and white casket. I remember my grandfather saying that he had spent over $10,000 on putting my mother away nicely and even dressing all five of us for her funeral. They made sure everything went well as far as the arrangement and getting us together.

Everyone was highly upset with my father for bringing his girlfriend to my mom's funeral. It was very disrespectful to my mother and her family. My father was trying to force us to kiss my mother goodbye, but I was too afraid of doing so, I didn't kiss her. My father was consistent and disappointed that we didn't. My grandfather carried me back where he was sitting. I looked across from him it was my mother's ex-boyfriend.

He had the nerve to come over to me as I was grieving my mother's death and said, "Please don't tell anyone what I did to you," and whatever my sister and I needed, to please give him a call. Everyone showed up and showed my mother the utmost respect. She was loved; she was 26 years old and had to leave 5 children behind. You would've thought my mom was a celebrity.

That night I laid in my bed thinking about my mother lying in that casket. I couldn't sleep at all. After the funeral, my father took us back to my grandmother's house and told us to pack all our stuff up; we were moving in with him. The next morning when we woke up, my father proceeded to tell us that his previous girlfriend was going to be our new mother. We should start calling her mother for now on. My sister and I said we would never call her mother. This woman was around my family and I always looked at her as my father's best friend wife. How disrespectful was that to my mother. He never left us alone with nobody before but family. He started leaving early in the morning and coming back late at night. He was becoming very irresponsible when it came to our care. He would allow his so-called future wife's daughter to kick and hit us; we were told not to fight back. So one day she kicked my little brother and then went to the kitchen to make a bowl of cereal. She turned back to get the milk, and my little brother poured a pile of sugar in her cereal. She started having diabetic seizures, she came out of the seizures and she was just fine. We grew tired of the mental and physical abuse by him leaving us there all the time. So just lying back waiting for my father to get home, my sister and I talked; She already got jumped by my aunts at my mother's funeral. My father was physically abusing her. He was not treating this woman right at all.

While all this was going on, I never told my father that my mother's boyfriend was molesting me. My sister told me that our mother's boyfriend was fondling her too. I sat back thinking that I should have told my father, to protect my sister and I.

I grabbed my sister and held her, telling her, "I got you, no more secrets between us. Let's make a promise, let's stick together like mother wanted us to do."

My sister was the oldest, but I was more mature than her by being up under my mother and other adults. My father returned home wondering where our mother was at (meaning his girlfriend). I knew that my mother was dead, so I ignored him. My little sister said she left with her daughter and she took their clothes.

He went in the other room to check and said, "She left, did she feed y'all?" "No, and we are hungry." So he said he would be right back; he was going to the store. He returned with some grocery and some White Castles. He went into the bathroom, I realized that my father was in the bathroom for a long while. I started knocking on the bathroom door but no response. I opened the door and saw my father on the toilet and he was very high out of it. I ran and called my aunt (my father's sister) and asked what I should do. She told me to put him in the tub and fill it with ice water to shock his body. I did exactly what she said. After he regained consciousness, he jumped up and left, leaving us there alone for three days with little food and diapers for my younger brother. I then went across the street and told my grandfather what was going on. They kept us with them for two days and took us back to my grandmother's house in Delray.

At this point everybody wanted us to be separated. My grandmother refused to let that happen. There was twelve of us living in a two-bedroom flat, with five to a bed, holes in the mattress and very dirty. By this time both my mother's parents started drinking heavily after the death of my mom.

Let me tell you the wonderful things about my grandmother the one who sacrifice and raised us. She came from a very rich family. She even had maids growing up as a little girl. My great-great- grandmother was from the Philippines. Despite her learning disabilities she was able to run a very successful business.

She raised eleven children plus the five of us; she was in love with my grandfather; she was a virgin and the first time they became intimate she became pregnant. She thought she was going to spend the rest of her life with him. She was devastated to find out that he had a child on the way. My grandfather decided to marry another woman instead of my grandmother. Since then she was slightly depressed. She went on with her life and dated other people and had other kids. My grandmother and grandfather still had a lot of love for each other because of my mother. He moved next door to help my grandmother with his wife at the time which was jealous of my grandmother and grandfather's relationship they shared.

My grandfather stopped helping my grandmother with us financially and started drinking alcohol heavily. The loss of my mother he became very depressed. My great-uncle (grandfather's brother) lived across from us; we all lived on the same street in Delray. My great-uncle and his wife didn't have any kids, so she took a liking to me. She would always find ways to help me make money by helping me find little odd jobs. My oldest sister was so miserable because of the poor conditions that we were living in. She started running away every chance she got. She would run to my daddy's older sister house in Ecorse. My grandmother would always call the police and they would always bring her back to Delray. She was always angry and dissatisfied of the way they treated us. Making us do all the cleaning and cooking. Taking care of my brothers and sister was not supposed to be like this; we woke up to a pure nightmare. I understood why my sister was trying to escape hell, but every time they brought her back. I would hold her and tell her I promised Mother that we would stick together no matter what. One day I will get us out these living conditions. I said, "I'm sorry, I'm going to make it right. I promise." I had a talk with my grandparents to make sure they were not going to separate us. My father's father was thinking of taking me and my oldest sister because he was about to get married and she already had nine children of her own and both of them worked. My father's oldest sister was financially secure. She owned a few businesses; my aunt only had two children, and she was taking care of my other aunt, which was my father's baby sister.

After my grandmother passed, my father's older sister would always take us shopping, buying us clothes, shoes, and anything that she thought we needed at the time. Every time we come back to my grandmother's, she made us share our clothes and shoes with her children. My aunt used to get so steamed about it. She asked us where the clothes and shoes she purchased for us when she picked us up for the weekend. One day my aunt begged my grandmother to give her custody of me and my siblings. My grandmother said no because she loved was getting government assistant at the time, it was helping her with survival for all of us. I believe my grandmother kept us 'cause we was the only memory she had of her daughter. My aunt wouldn't be able to handle all five of us. My aunt went over to talk to my father who had full custody of me and my siblings. My father was too upset with his sister and he was too strung out on drugs he said no. They kept falling out about how he handled their mother's estate. My father used to call my grandmother and tell her that he wanted his kids or to give him some money. That was the rumor but I don't know that to be true. Playing mind games so he could use the money to can get high. My grandmother loved all of her children and would do anything she could to keep us all together. He knew that would hurt my grandmother to be departed from us. He would play mind games with my oldest sister to meet him down at the corner. He had a new bike for her. I can remember one day my sister sat outside waiting on my father all day and night. Finally I told her that our father was hooked on drugs and he was not the same father as we once knew. He wouldn't allow us to live in these types of conditions. A whole year passed since we saw my dad.

One day returning home from school, my grandmother was telling us we were going to stay with my father for the weekends. He has been in rehab and supposed to be off drugs. "By law, I cannot stop him from seeing y'all. That's your father. So y'all will be spending the weekend with him." The weekend came, and he picked us up; we were so happy to see our father. He took us shopping; he was getting his life in order and he was able to purchase a home on the east side. I was so proud of him. He told me and my sister, thirteen and twelve at the time, we can help take care of my other brothers and sisters while he went to work because he was a supervisor for the city and he had the house all set up for us. Even with his addiction he maintained his supervisor position with the city. He was going to get us back from our grandmother and he shouldn't never have left his children, and how much he loved & missed us. My oldest sister and I told my father that it's okay. We know you were hurting losing your mother and our mother, what pain that must have been." He looked at me and said, "You know, you just like your mother, with an old soul. He would always come to me to find out information on what is going on in the family." He said, "What's your grandmother's favorite line?" "Kings and queens fall down. Never look down on a man unless you are picking him up."

We all said it at the same time, remembering this was what my mother used to say. "Never look down on anyone." We were happy that our father was back in our lives and off of drugs. Everything was going good for six months. Visiting our father every weekend. Then he went from one addiction to another. He started drinking for the first time. I was afraid of him because one night my sister and I were up talking with my father about becoming young ladies, starting our menstrual cycle. I felt very uncomfortable talking to him about it when he was drinking. When we went to bed that night, I told my sister to help me block the bedroom door so he couldn't get in without us knowing. She said, "You know Daddy is going to beat our butt if he can't get in."

So early the next morning he came to check on us and he realized that he couldn't get into the room he said, "Y'all get up and put your robes on and come into the living room so we can talk."

He sat us down and hugged us and said he would never harm us in a sexual way. I was still afraid because of what I had been through with my mother's boyfriend fondling me and my sister. I didn't know how to tell him the change that took place in my female body. My oldest sister said that she already started to go through her cycle too. He said he noticed that our bodies started developing into young ladies. My sister said dad "that's why we needed to be with you to help us get the things we need". Grandmother couldn't help us with the personal things and clothes we needed. She could barely take care of her own children. I told my father that my sister and I would help him to raise my siblings. It was important that we all stay with him. "Please keep us. You can go to work and don't have to worry about a thing. We need to be a family; the house is perfect for that." I can remember saying that. God, no more roaches because my father was a neat freak. No roaches in the cereals and no holes in the mattress. Once I looked in my siblings' eyes realizing that we were happy to be back with my dad and he was very excited too.

The next day being Sunday, we had to pack up and get ready to go back to Granny's. Mind you, I love my grandmother, and she was doing the best she could for us and for her own kids without any support from their fathers. She was mourning the death of her daughter. She started drinking heavily, never leaving the house; she was miserable, and had a very abusive boyfriend. I can remember waking up one morning to my mother's oldest brother coming in and finding my grandmother's boyfriend jumping on her; my uncle picked up a rifle and pistol whipped him, almost killing him. He ran out of the room butt naked and blood was everywhere. It was crazy until I saw my grandmother's face; her boyfriend had broken her nose. He jumped into his car naked saying he was going to get a gun. He was known for always carrying a gun. My grandmother was very angry with my uncle for jumping on her boyfriend; she still called the police to protect my uncle because her boyfriend was coming back with a gun. The police caught him while he was on his way back to my grandmother's house. He was sentenced to two years for the gun charge. My grandmother loved him so much; she would send him letters and put money on his books. I said to myself that I would never love any man like that. She was crying all the time while he was gone and playing this song called "Before I Cut You a Loose." She kept it on repeat.

At this time we haven't heard from my father in a while, so I made it up in my mind that I had to do what I had to do. My siblings and I would make it through this ordeal. At the age of twelve during the summer months, I started a cleaning service. Going around cleaning all the elder people's houses on our street. I also helped a lady at the Salvation Army unloading boxes when they came in. She offered to give me clothes. I would have first pick of all new arrivals of clothing for me and my family. I was so tired of eating beans without any meat or corn bread.

On the corner where we lived there was a young man; he was fifteen years of age. I was twelve. His mother ran the numbers on the block, so he always had money and drove his mom's car. One day he saw me and my little brother walking back from the market. He was so kind to offer us a ride; by it being too cold, I accepted the ride. He started telling me about how much he liked me and he would do anything for me. He said he would help me with my siblings, so I said, "If you really like me I would love to have some meat to eat. All were eating is beans. He Laughed." I told him, "I'm a virgin, and I'm not having sex because my grandmother would kill me." She was always taking us to the doctor to get us checked out to see if we were having sex. The doctor would always tell her that they couldn't examine us because of our age. She was so afraid that history would repeat itself, terrified that one day we would get pregnant at a young age like my mother. He would buy me really nice gifts, and he used to give his brother hand-me-downs to my little brothers. It's funny one day he took out all the meat from his mother's freezer and brought it to me. The next day, his mother came down to my grandmother's house and asked, "Did my son bring some meat down here to give to your granddaughter? He really loves that girl. I always see her sitting on the porch talking to him. My son told me one day he will wait for her to get older so he can pursue her. For now she is just a good friend, that family needs my help." He explained to his mother that he would pay her back for the meats out of his Social Security check that he was receiving every month.

Still no words from my father; he had gone away again. I was telling my friend that my grandmother could only afford to buy us two outfits apiece and one pair of shoes for going back to school clothes. I went into the money I was saving to buy some more clothes for us for school.

RELEASE

My first week in high school, I tested very low for the 9th grade; they wanted me to enroll in the special education classes. My older sister showed me around the high school and how to sign up for the free lunch program. When I was giving the woman my information for the free lunch program, this young man that was standing behind me heard my birthday and said, "That's my birthday date as well." When I turned around and saw him, he looked into my eyes and I adored his nice smile. Then eventually, he asked me for my number. I felt happy because he was very popular. He was drummer in the school band, not to mention how fine he was with an outstanding personality. My sister told me that he was a player, and to be careful. He also messed around with a couple of girls in Delray. She didn't want me to date him at all. She always thought she was my protector.

Later that day, I met another guy; he was two years older than me. He used to tease me on how I smelled like butter. My grandmother used to press our hair with old oil, she had on the stove. He would always say "you and your sister got rocking bodies", even though I was flat-chested. My sister had a banging body; she was popular throughout Southwestern. In fact, she dated the varsity quarterback of the football team. I just had one male friend in Delray who lived down on the corner from me. I don't know why I was a late bloomer, but I was very mature for my age. Knowing that all boys wanted to have sex, I wasn't going to be like most women I knew that was having sex at this age. I didn't want to be buck wild.

My grandmother started allowing my sister to go on dates. I can remember one night in particular; it was two o'clock in the morning, and our curfew was at twelve. I began to worry. I told my grandmother to call the police because my sister probably ran away again. The police told me to describe what my sister had on, soon as I started describing her she suddenly walked up. I grabbed and hugged her, saying I thought she had run away. She said her friend's mother's car broke down, but I knew that was a lie. My sister knew she still would be put on punishment. When we were getting ready for bed, I asked her to tell me the truth. She told me that she had lost her virginity to the school's quarterback. I asked her, "Did it hurt?" She said "no!, "I think I love him," I laughed and said, "You don't know what love is, you know you have periods and you can get pregnant?" She told me "shut up" we started laughing and fell asleep. To our surprise she was pregnant from her first intimate moment.

In the morning my godfather came over to visit my grandmother, telling her he hit the lottery and he bought a flat in River Rouge. Right now I have a tenant that lives upstairs, and that we could move into the lower flat as soon as he got done painting, with no deposit. He told me he had a job for me helping a man disabled wife who live next door to the flat we were going to be shortly moving in. She needed light assistance; all I could say was thank you, God. Finally we could get out of stinky Delray. I was excited about the good news. I couldn't wait to get to school to tell my boyfriend. I would be moving to River Rouge and ask how far it was from where he stayed in Southwest Detroit. When I asked, he said six to eight blocks away from him. I thought to myself, wow! He must be the one for me, because I miss him while we were out on summer break although we talked on the phone all the time. He never pressured me to have sex, more like a great friend and mentor. My friend Abel was in tears when he found out we were moving out of Delray. He just lived over the bridge not that far away from me. He said all his family lived in River Rouge and Delray. "I would visit often because you're so pretty and you gone need me to protect you like I always do." I was so excited about the good news. I knew he would protect me, because he always did against the other boys. He was attracted to my personality and my strong will. I think he was really feeling sorry for the poor living situation that I was in.

My sister was upset because she didn't want to move out of Delray. She was in love with the quarterback that stayed in Delray. I started to notice how he started treating my sister after sleeping with her. He treated her with no respect. Trying to jump on her, he was very abusive. We moved to River Rouge; my sister said she thought she was pregnant. "You only fifteen years old, what do you know about being a mother?" She said, "I'm having my baby with no support from the child's father." He claimed that the baby wasn't his and she wasn't pregnant by him. "I told her don't worry about him I was employed at the time I got your back".

RELEASE

    The man finally moved out from the upstairs flat. I asked my godfather, "Can my sister and I rent the upstairs flat?" He said yes; my sister and I started to decorate. The man I worked for next door gave me some used furniture that he had in the basement. I cleaned it up and put plastic on it. As much as I tried to keep the upstairs clean the downstairs flat still was infected with roaches. My baby sister used to always come upstairs to sleep with me while she sucked her thumbs, crying, saying she missed her mother. I would tell her everything will be ok, I would do my best to take care of us, we cried ourselves to sleep. Holding on, saying God why we had to go through so much pain at a young age, feeling like I never had a chance to be a kid, with four kids to take care of. I felt overwhelmed with responsibilities. My oldest sister was the protector, and I was the provider being 14 helping my grandmother too. I was determined to provide everything my siblings and I needed. We had no support from none of my family members at this time. I took criticism from all the girls in the neighborhood. I was even accused of sleeping with the old man I worked for. That wasn't true he used to talk and mentor me helping me through life, telling me, "Don't get pregnant, wait till you get married, you see how hard it is on your sister without any support from the father. Look at what she is going through and learn from her." He used to say to me, "Why buy the cow if you can get the milk for free?" It was an old saying that meant why get married if you're already playing house. "Stop letting people put you down because of your unfortunate situation. Your mother passed and your father became addicted to heroin, that's not your fault. Just keep your head up, stay strong, and keep taking care of your siblings." He went to talk to my grandmother, telling her that he appreciated me for helping with his wife and thanked her for trusting me to do so. I really enjoyed being over there; it was a good learning experience and kept money in my pocket every week. His wife told me that she was going to leave me in her will. One time she gave me her credit card to go Christmas shopping to get my family some clothes from Sears and not to go over one thousand dollars, and her brother took me. I remember thinking, thank God for this lady; everything was coming together for me and my siblings. Everything was going to be just fine; it was the best Christmas ever. The smile on my siblings' faces was my Christmas gift. The last few years they were getting a good fellow box only.

The love of my life had taken me to meet his family a month before. Such a loving family they were; they accepted me with love and kindness. He used to bring leftover food from his job for us to help out; he worked for Burger King at the time. My siblings adored him, especially my little brothers. They would always catch the bus with him downtown on Saturday to watch martial arts movies at the Fox Theater. I felt very blessed to have him in my life. He was a good listener and had a lot of patience with me. All the girls in high school wanted him, but he still had quality time for me and my family. He still never pressured me to have sex, we just enjoyed each other company. I was virgin at the time, and I knew he could have sex with any girl at any time. Just didn't want to be another notch on his belt. I was too afraid of getting pregnant. I wanted to make sure he wanted me for me. We developed a good friendship and a special bond. After dating for a long time, I decided I wasn't going to listen to any of the girls at school. One Saturday at the movies, I sat my brothers in front of me so I can see them. Him and I sat in the back; we were kissing, and I told him to pull his pant down, and I started kissing all over him. He said, "Wow." I felt I had to do that to give him something to hold on to. Boy, he was excited; and I told him that would be his special treat.

As time went, he would see me in the hall at school and ask me why I wasn't in class, knowing I was too embarrassed to tell him I was put in special educational class. He had big plans for the future. He wanted to go to college and become a designer/musician. I remember one day he called me excited about being in battle of the bands, and he needed some new shoes. His parents couldn't afford them, so I told him to come on over. Knowing it was so important to him, when he got over to my house, I told him, "Let's go downtown, we caught the bus." When we got there, I brought him a pair of black and white Stacey Adams. I went against what the old man told me, "Never buy a man shoes, or anything, they will walk right out of your life." I never believed in that superstition. I thought I found my soul mate. I would do anything I could to help him. He was always there for me and my family, we shared the same birthday, I felt like we had a great bond.

I never dealt with many females. I couldn't trust them. So I kept my two male friends that knew my boyfriend, and they all lived on the same block to my surprise. I never saw them together because one of my male friends was a few years older than us. He used to call me at night and come over to play cards with me, he treated me like his little sister; that was the bond we shared. I knew his most intimate secrets and he knew mine. He knew how I felt about my boyfriend; he used to tell me all about his friends and all the girls they use to run game on. He used to tell me that I was wasting my time with my boyfriend. He don't like you he like this other girl. I told him I didn't care; we weren't having sex. They both were very popular at school; my older male friend had won class best dressed. He always kept himself together. One particular girl I met knew my boyfriend, and she liked him. I found out. He called her his little play sister. Her and I became real good friends, my male friend told me that my boyfriend brought her around to spy on me. I didn't think that because her family treated me so nicely. My male friend started telling me how he felt about me, and I told him no way. "I know how you treat women, and we're just friends. I asked him if he would teach me how to dress. He said no problem; when he got his first check, he took me to get my hair done. He bought me a new outfit. I was sharp, most definitely a brick house. I said, "I cannot wait for my boyfriend to see me."

It was our birthday the next day. I recall buying us a birthday cake and taking it to school. You should've seen the smile on his face; that's all I needed to make me happy on our birthday. He made me believe in love again. He was complimenting me on how beautiful I looked. That was the best birthday since my mother passed.

My sister gave birth to a little boy; when she came home from the hospital, I had everything set up for her and her newborn baby. I was right there when he was born, trying to show my sister I was her support. Thought we had a great bond until one night I was babysitting for my sister and my auntie at my aunt house and I had to take my nephew with me. My sister didn't come in time she called and told me that my nephew's father would be picking him up over at our aunt's house. When he came to pick up my nephew he started making sexual passes toward me. Telling me that he should've chose me because I was so mature for my age. He always wanted me. I immediately grabbed the house phone and called my grandmother and told her what happened. He picked up my nephew and left my aunt's house. My grandmother told me to never tell my sister; it would come in between us. Then she found out she was pregnant with her second child. I told my grandmother I was telling my sister exactly what happened because we said that we wouldn't keep any secrets from each other. We had been through a whole lot together. I wouldn't let any man come in between us. I cried and prayed all night on my decision to tell my sister that her baby father had made sexual passes toward me.

The next day I returned home thinking what I did to make him disrespect me like that. I always handled myself with respect and I started blaming myself because my sister was so in love with him, and about to have their second child. I never wanted her to be hurt, by telling her what happened but I needed to. So I went to talk to one of my male friends about it. He told me to tell my sister exactly what happened. If she found out she would think that I wanted him. It would destroy our relationship, so I did tell her. I told her exactly what happened. She was crying, telling me that he was a dog because he had another child on the way by another girl from school. He had broken up with her. I thought to myself, good, she deserved better and had a gang of guys that loved her. She was beautiful; she could have anyone.

As time went on, our relationship became stronger, and he told me not to listen to what other people tell me about him. As long as he got my ear, never come to him with what they say. Just trust what we had. I would never waste our time on arguing. I just wanted to enjoy the quality time we spent together. It came a time when I was going to give myself to him. We planned it out, and I was going to his house. I was so afraid to give myself to him because I was still a virgin. When I got there, he started kissing my neck. He already knew that whenever he kissed me, he got excited, so he was very gentle with me. I felt the warmth of me coming, or was it just the blood all over his sheets? I felt so embarrassed that I bled all over his sheets. He said it's okay; he would take care of it. He took me home; he had a smile on his face while he was holding me saying goodbye. I told him not to discuss our sexual business with anyone and to keep his promise. He was pretty good at keeping his promises. Every chance we got, we had sex, and boy, I enjoyed it. Afterward we would lay in each other's arms talk and tell each other how we feel about each other.

Months went by; his family just bought a new car, and he told me that he was going to take me out and not on the bus this time. I was so happy; he was the only man I wanted to be intimate with. We were getting ready for our date, I was waiting for him to pull up. I had to run next door to get my paycheck from my patient. I told my sister to tell him I would be right back. When he pulled up, I wasn't in there no longer than five minutes, and he was banging on the door. He said, "What are you doing in there?" I replied "I had to get my pay check". He walked me back home and said, "I will see you another time." I said, "What happen to our date; how all of a sudden we not going?" He said he had to take his parents' car back. I said okay. I never forgot the expression on my sister's face when I went in the house. She said, "Oh, what happened, y'all not going out tonight?" That's when she said, "What's the matter, they all do that after they have sex with you, they play you to the left."

He started to hang out with this one particular girl she was a cheerleader. I went up to him and asked about the promise we made to each other. "What happen to your promise, if you wanted to date someone I would be the first to know. He said he would be over when he got off work tonight and we would talk. When he came over around nine that night, we had sex, and he told me that he wanted to be with the cheerleader at school. I held back my tears and said okay, and he said, "We will always be friends." I said, "No, thank you."

Feeling like a fool, I cried myself to sleep that night. The next day I went downstairs to talk to my aunt, saying to her I did everything for him, gave myself to him and supported him in everything he did. My aunt said to me, "If a man doesn't want you anymore, there is nothing you can do about it" and, "Is it the same girl he brought over here saying she is his sister?" I said no.

She said, "He is not the only guy that likes you, you have good male friends." What about that one boy. I can't date my friends old boyfriend. She said but, "He's always over, and he will do anything for you. He takes you shopping, and he's always there for you." I said, "I don't love him and don't like the way he treats girls. I could never like him. I am in love with my boyfriend. I just would find a way to get over him."

I asked my grandmother if I could attend River Rouge night school, so I wouldn't have to see him at school again and with other girls. It hurt too much. My grandmother said okay as long as I was in school; she didn't care. So the next day I went to school to clean out my locker and to talk to a good friend of mine. She held me and said, "I told you, all the boys wants to do is have sex with you and on to the next." and, "I never like you hanging with his play sister."

On our way leaving school, we ran into my ex-boyfriend at his locker, kissing his new girlfriend. The last time I saw my ex-friend was three weeks ago. He came over to my house very angry, accusing me of messing around with our so-called friend. I told him he had a lot of nerve to ask me anything.

"Don't you have a new girlfriend?" He said, "Every night, my friends and I hang out, he always finds a reason to go home. But I heard that he's been coming over to see you." I told him, "Yes, he does, he's just my friend." I said, "What do you need?" He said that he loved me. He was sorry for how things went down, but she was a cheerleader and we're always hang out together. He said it didn't matter whom I was with. He grabbed me, and we got into a struggle. He pulled out a pocket knife and cut me three times, yelling, "I love you." Not knowing that I was cut, I went back into the house, removing my coat. My uncles at the table noticed that I was bleeding and asked me what happened. "Was that your boyfriend outside?" I said yes.

My uncle immediately jumped up and ran outside and brought him back to my grandmother's house. He started asking me if he cut me. I told them, "No, we were wrestling, and I fell and hurt myself." I wanted to protect him, and I knew my uncles would've really hurt him. They were very protective over the women in the family. They weren't raised to hit women. After my ex-boyfriend left, my aunt called me in her bedroom." She wanted to examine me and check the cuts on my arm. She told me I might need some stitches; the cuts were pretty deep. She knew I was afraid of needles, so I said that's okay. She said, "Did he cut you? That look like a cut." I said, "No, I fell."

Later on that evening my friend came over, and I was in my room crying. He said, "What's wrong?" I started to tell him about what happened between me and my ex-boyfriend, he said, "Let me check out your arm." When he saw the cuts, he said, "He would never do that, it's not his personality." I said, "He did do it because he thought that you and I were messing around behind his back."

He started busting out laughing, saying, "I heard he dumped you after he bust your cherry, bragging about how you been spending money on him." My friend said, "I told you that he was a player." "Hurry and get dressed, because if that really happen to you, we are going to his house. We are going to show his parents what he has done." I said, "No, I'm not going over there. I'm going to change schools so I can never see him again. I thought he really loved me for him to cut me based on hearsay. I know he has to be hurting for him to do that to me."

My friend said, "You so stupid, he been bragging about taking another girl to the prom." I said, "That's all good." He was going away to college and his family was moving out of town, so I said, "I'm done talking about it." I said, "I want you to leave."

Later on that night, I received a phone call telling me that he was at the picnic with his new girl. My girlfriend said, "I'm glad you're done with him." She said, "Are you crying?" I said, "I should have listened to you and my grandmother, you all were right. Once you give yourself to a man, you cannot take it back."

Then she started asking me why I haven't been back at school. I told her I wasn't coming back to that school. She told me she would be over tomorrow. The next day, she came over and noticed that my arm was wrapped up, and she asked me what happened.

I told her what happened, and she said, "What you are going to do about it?" She said, "After all, he quit you and cut you." I said, "It's okay, I'm done with men." The pain felt like when I lost my mother; this really hurt. I was devastated. But through it all, my male friend kept checking on me, coming over practically every day asking me to give him another chance, telling me that he would be there for me, taking me shopping—anything to make me smile. One thing led to another. I was at my Aunts babysitting, and we ended up messing around. God knows I needed a friend. I was feeling so down, not blaming him for my actions, but when I laid down with him, I felt worse—worse about me, feeling embarrassed, knowing that I didn't love him. I was still in love with my ex. There's no turning back now. I sat down and talked to my aunt about it, and she said, "You love too hard. It's best for you to find a man that loves you.

The following month, I had missed my period, went to the doctor, and found out I was pregnant. I went to my grandmother and asked her if I could move out on my own. She said, "Yes, you been on your own for a while." I told her I had a lot of money saved for my first place. Now 18 and pregnant, I moved out on my own, my oldest sister telling me that I could stay with her because she knew I would be a big help to her and the kids. That's the only reason why she wanted me to stay with her. Telling my new boyfriend that I was pregnant, he said he never wanted any kids. So unsure if it was his or my ex. I didn't care what he had to say. I was keeping my baby. I knew it was a chance it wasn't his baby. I was determined to hold on to my child. So nothing or nobody could make me give up my precious baby. I told him it was my decision, and I was holding on because I knew my child would be a great blessing to me. Cause the first time I had sex I got pregnant. I never told anyone and I reached out to one of my close friends. She took to have an abortion. He was still at the plant, and my ex and his family was about to move to Atlanta Georgia and going away to college. I asked him to help move me to a better place for me and my child. It was no problem with

RELEASE

him helping me move. I had the deposit and two months' rent saved. I had worked up to the eighth month of my pregnancy.

One day my sister called me to tell me about a party. She asked me to come and go with her so I can have some fun, since I haven't been out in a while with her. I said, "Yes, I will go with you." But my main focus at the moment was on me and my unborn child. When I got there, all I did was sit there and watch people dance. Then I saw my boyfriend there at the party. He said, "Sit right here. I will go and get you something to eat. Don't you try to dance."

I knew how slick he was just like clockwork. He was walking out with another girl. I got up from the chair where I was sitting and started fighting through the crowd to follow him. He went straight to his car with the young lady. They were kissing. I knocked on the window, and I realized I had seen her before, he jumped out of his car, trying to explain to me that she didn't mean anything to him. The young lady started telling me that he was lying, that they were messing around for a few years. She started telling me that he said he didn't want me and saying that the child I was carrying wasn't his, and how, "He used to go over to your house to see your uncle, not you." I immediately went over to him and started swinging, crying, saying, "I made a terrible mistake. God, please forgive me." He was a very selfish person; all he wanted to do was have sex with me. So by this time, my sister was coming out of the party. She was walking up to him, saying, "You better not put your hands on her." He said, "Tell her to stop hitting on me." I stopped and got in the car with my sister, riding home telling her that God don't like ugly.

I blame myself for messing with him. She said, "Don't blame yourself, you will be a wonderful mother. You're already a wonderful aunt." I went back to the apartment; the next day he came to my apartment knocking on my door. He apologized, saying, "I told you that the girl meant nothing to me." My baby was due next month, so I let him come back. He slept on the couch, knowing I had no desire for him. I didn't want to be alone. I was afraid I was going to have my baby at any moment now. She was born in the middle of April; The next day I met this old Polish woman who asked me to follow her home. When we got there, the old lady gave me two thousand dollars, she started telling me that my baby would bring me thousands of blessings. I was all in tears saying to myself that I had to forgive myself for the mistake that I have made. God doesn't make any mistakes.

When I made it home, I got a phone call; it was my long-lost father whom I haven't heard from in a few years. Telling me he heard that I was pregnant and he wanted to be there for me. Then he dropped a bomb, telling me that he had a child on the way too. My father kept his word, and he bought me a bassinet filled with a whole lot of baby stuff. He came to the hospital to visit his granddaughter when she was born. I was very happy that he kept his word. Then all the nurses in the hospital started asking me where my baby's father was because she looked like she had some Indian in her, she was so beautiful and had long pretty curly hair. She was the love of my life; Born in April, and I named her April. My favorite song was "My April Love." I had to have a C-section, so I needed my boyfriend for assistance around the house. We both started gaining weight, I was miserable and he was too. He started drinking heavily and hanging out with his friends. He started cheating with one of the women at his job. I held on to him; it was important to me that my baby had a father in her life because my father wasn't there for me. But the longer I held on to him, I was losing more and more of myself.

My baby got sick and was hospitalized, his mother and sister came to the hospital saying that I was an unfit mother. She had asthma, they told me they could give my baby a better life if I gave them custody. I told them I would never give my baby up. I carried her for nine months, his mother was always judgmental about me in a negative way. He said that his mother just thought we were too young for kids, and she thought she could raise her better. He asked me to give my baby to his mother because she wanted him to go back to school to better his life.

One night I asked him to drop my sister and I at skating; while we were there one of my friends tripped and fell on my ankle and broke it. I had to call my boyfriend back to take me to the hospital. He came back drunk, and while we were on our way to the hospital, we got into a car accident. My family met us there, my aunt asked me if we had full coverage insurance. I said yes and she said the insurance company would give me twenty dollars a day for someone to come and help me around the house.

Six months had gone by, and we were waiting on the insurance check. My aunt came over the one who informed us about the insurance company, and she asked me if I received the check for household services yet. I told her no. That's when she said, "Let's call the insurance company and find out why you haven't received it." But to my surprise, the check had been issued out two months prior. I hung up with them and called my boyfriend to ask him if his mother received the check. He straight up lied and said no. I got off the phone with him and decided to call his mother to ask her about the check. When she answered, I asked her and, she started going off on me, telling me that the check didn't belong to me, I told her we had an agreement. "You told me that you didn't want any of the money, to keep it." Her son and I were struggling at the time. She went on screaming and yelling at me until my aunt took the phone and said, "Shame on you, how can you take from the mother of your grandkid?"

She started telling my aunt that I was nothing and I didn't work, so my aunt hung up the phone and wanted to go over there. I told her, "No, I will wait till her son gets here and make him handle his mother." Out of respect for him, and she was my kid grandmother. He came home that night still lying about the check, saying it never came. I told him that I called the insurance company and they said the check had been cashed by me and his mother. Someone had to sign my name; he started to tell me that he paid the insurance and whatever his mother said goes.

At the time we were living in a two-bedroom apartment and expecting our second child. We were going to take the check and find a bigger place for the kids and my younger siblings. Only to get messed over in the end. I was expecting that money to purchase a house and get on our feet. Mind you, my boyfriend's mother never did any work to get the check. But here she goes, deciding to keep all the money for herself. What hurt the most was my kid father knew she had received the check and signed my name on it. I didn't find out until thirty days later. He was the one who signed my name on the check. Mad and upset, I told my boyfriend that if he couldn't stand up to his mother for me and our kids, he wasn't the man for me. I left him after I saved enough money for me and my kids to move.

It was a three-bedroom ranch house on the west side of Detroit; I was determined to show him and his mother that I could stand on my own without their help. I took a lot of disrespect from his mother and wasn't taking it anymore. Come to find out my boyfriend's sister called and told me that her mother was money-hungry. She did the same thing to her and her husband too. I was planning to take my siblings; my youngest brother was giving my grandmother problems. I promised her; she could keep the check she was receiving for them and, she agreed they could come live with me.

At the time my youngest brother was eleven. Him and his friends were playing next door to the grocery store. They started playing with a pellet gun, trying to shoot tires out on cars. The pellet gun had missed the tires and accidently hit a little girl in the back of her head; she was sitting in the car, and it killed her. Next thing we heard was the police and helicopters all around shutting down the whole area because the little girl was killed. They went house to house, asking questions about the shooting. I always knew when my little brother had done something wrong. His hands started sweating, and he got this look on his face. He started saying, "Man, it was blood all over the back seat of that car." My brother did not say who did it because of his loyalty to his friends. He started saying, "I'm not a snitch." I told him he better tell me what happened before they take him to jail. He said, "he didn't know what happened."

The next day I received a call from my grandmother, telling me a couple of FBI agents were at the house to take her and my little brother down to ask a few questions about the murder. I told my grandmother I would meet them there. I got down to the station; my grandmother was standing in the lobby, and I saw my brother's friend parents. The agents told my grandmother that he and his friends were out there at that time of the shooting. Hours went by; my little brother kept quiet, but his friend admitted to what happened. It was an accident; they were just trying to shoot at the tires, not kill anyone. They sentenced my brother's friend to serve years in juvenile detention, and my brother wasn't charged for anything. They immediately released him, I told my grandmother I was taking him with me. He never had to see this place again.

At the time, my father and both my grandfathers were nowhere around. My father's father had retired and moved down south. He used to help us out a lot, now no support at all. I was planning to move on the west side of Detroit. I threatened to go to his mother's church and tell the pastor what she had done to me and my kids.

I was at the Laundromat washing all of our clothes, getting ready to move into my new place. I met this older gentleman. I was in tears over the situation. He saw me crying, and he walked over to me and started asking me why I was crying. He said he was going through a situation and he needed help with his grandmother. He asked me if I was interested in a job taking care of her. I immediately said "yes". He told me, "Stop crying", I will do the best I can for you and your children." God knows he was a blessing. I helped him with his grandmother, and he helped with my kids. I also helped him build his credit. He had a girlfriend at the time who was taking all of his money every payday. He was the only child and well taken care of. His mother just passed and left him a nice piece of money. He never had kids of his own. I always knew that God sent him to me at the right time. He would always tell me, "Don't worry about a thing. If the kid's father comes over let him see them. Please don't keep them away."

My kid's father came to get them every weekend, telling me he wanted his family back. I told him that I wasn't coming back, he broke down and said, "Let's get married." He said his mother would respect me then. I knew then I couldn't marry him because he was doing it just to please her. That was his main concern, he was still messing around with one of the women from his job too. I cannot say he was a horrible guy; we were just young. We started the relationship wrong. I was at the time in my life where I wanted to have fun and was into younger guys. He was always very jealous of my older friends.

RELEASE

My little brother always thought of his sister as his mother figure. They were very protective of me and my sisters. One day we were in the living room, and the guy I was dating pushed me. My baby brother jumped up and beat the guy up and threw him out the window. We were very happy living in our new home, waking up and not smelling the horrible scent of the dog factory. Finally I was free of my nightmare of living in southwest Detroit and all the terrible things that happened to me. I still found myself sad and lonely. Thank God for my older friend; he was so supportive to me and my family. He always been a replacement grandfather and father in our lives (God is Good). He brought me my first car.

One day I received a phone call, my sister screaming, telling me to get to my grandmother's house now. My aunt and grandmother were into a heated argument over my grandmother's man. In the heat of the argument, my aunt said, "While everyone was judging and belittling me about sleeping with my mother's man. She said tell your grandchildren the truth "you been lying all this time, you played a part in your daughter death. If you don't believe me, ask your grandmother how your mother really died." All this time we were told her gloss Stones erupted. My brother didn't understand, so my aunt threw the death certificate, and told my brother, "You so smart, read this." As my brother was reading, my grandmother started screaming and crying. My aunt then started explaining what happened. She said that my mother was pregnant at the time and had hemorrhaged to death. My mother had got pregnant, she didn't know who the father was. She wanted my father back so she proceeded to get which was illegal back then an abortion. My brother called our siblings, over the news of my mother's death a huge fight broke out. My oldest sister fought my aunt. By the time I arrived, my sister and aunts were still fighting. I ran in the house to see if my grandmother was okay. She was screaming and crying, saying how much she loved her daughter and how my mother asked her to support her decision.

My grandmother and my mother had a very tight bond with each other. She knew that my mother wanted to go back to my father. She never meant for this to happen. So at this point, the truth finally came out about how my mother died. Being a mother at this time, I understood why my grandmother would start drinking a lot and locking herself in her room for hours. She couldn't deal with what happened; my grandmother and I always had a very close relationship. That's why if she were still around today, I wouldn't be able to tell this story. She had suffered enough. To bury a child was very devastating to my grandparents. They both became heavy drinkers. My oldest sister felt that my grandmother should have treated us better, knowing how my mother really died. My father knew the truth the whole time. He put her under pressure to make that decision; that's why he couldn't be around us. Wow, all these secrets, she would have never had abortions knowing this. We were lied to about how my mother died, how devastating! My grandfather, my mother's father, never knew the truth until we told him. We all were hurting in pain over the loss; wish we had known. My sister was telling my grandmother how she hated them and she wanted to hit my grandmother, but she knew better. She started taking pictures off the wall and tearing them up. We were in her room crying, and I told her, "I can only imagine how she feels. I know you never would have hurt your child purposely. I know you were trying to help her." "I love you very much, and thanks for keeping us together." Even though I was heartbroken, crying, thinking about the sacrifice she had made for a man that was not supportive of his children at the end.

They never told the doctor she had an illegal procedure, and she started hemorrhaging and it was too late for my mother. It was against the law in the seventies, aborting children, not knowing she was having twins at the time. Now I looked at my siblings, I saw all the damage and pain it put in our lives. Life was hell without her. Sitting here talking to her father. Him telling me the reason why they didn't say anything; because back then, they sent people to jail for having abortions. He said, "Wow, they didn't let him know either, all these secrets." He said, "No man shouldn't have to bury his children." He already lost a son and daughter. With tears running down his face, I told him, "You have to hold on to your grandchildren. That's what you have left of your daughter."

From that day, our bond was even tighter than before; he gave up drinking, and I made sure he had a chance to bond with my children and my younger siblings. He was amazed at how my younger brother and I favored him. Telling me that he could always count on me to find him and I told him that he was the only thing we had left of my mother. Only thing we had left was my grandparents. He used to tell me stories of my mother when she was growing up as a kid. How smart, kind, and respectful she was. He was showing me pictures of how beautiful she was, as well with long wavy hair. Asking me why I cut my hair so short. He asked me to do him a favor and let my hair grow back. Telling me that my hair was my glory. I explained to him that my ex-boyfriend adored my long hair and at the time I had gained so much weight. I thought I looked better with my hair short.

    I asked him to do me a favor and get my younger brother into the plant where he was working. My other brother was in college to be an accountant. My younger brother was smart as well, but he needed some mentoring after the accidental death of the little girl. He was a very laid-back person until you provoked him. Whenever he made any money, he shared it with his family. One day he came into the house and asked me if I saw the news today. I replied no; he said in the west side of Detroit six people got shot. I noticed his hands were sweating. I asked him if he had anything to do with it. He was gathering up some of his things really fast. Telling me if the police came to me, tell them that I hadn't seen him. I told him I been in and out of the juvenile system with you. I now had my own children to take care of. He was already on probation, and this would be violating it. They would send him to prison. Looking at my brother, I noticed some bruises on his face. He told me he wasn't going to let anyone hurt him or our family. Watching the news that night, I heard that seven people got shot on the west side of Detroit. Two people died and five wounded. My brother was always staying with one of his siblings so the detective didn't know where to locate him. The next day, I had a visit from a few detectives, asking me when was the last time I saw my brother. I told them I hadn't seen him. Then they asked me, "Did he leave anything behind?" I said no, and they said, "We have him in custody on a murder charge." I asked him,

RELEASE

"Can I come down to the station with him?" He said, "Yes, on regular visiting hours."

I was waiting on my other brother to return home from school so I could tell him what happened. My sisters, already knew. The detective had been to their home as well. He was charged in the case but had a lot of love and respect on the streets. So no one testified against him; he beat the murder case. He ended up going to jail for violating his probation. He did seven years for his violent temper when he only should had done two years. His parole officer would ask him would what would you do if a pink elephant start flying around the room. He would say I would shoot it, "they would hold him back every time.

My family and I supported him while he was in lockdown. We didn't want him to have to ask for nothing while he was in prison. My brother told me that my father was accepting collect calls from him and sending money. No matter where he was, I always supported him by keeping him encouraged by visiting him. I told him I was getting tired of going back and forth to prison to see him. He promised me he was done.

My older brother told me after he graduated and was working at the bank he wasn't happy with his job. He was moving to West Virginia and opening up a hair salon with one of his friends. I can just remember thinking how hard it was being separated from my brothers who always loved and protected me; our bond was priceless.

I started messing back around with this young guy my younger brother had a fight with. It was the worst thing I could have done. He knew my brothers weren't around to protect me, and then he became very violent and jealous of my older male friends. So I ended the relationship with him, then one night my oldest daughter was sick. My kid's father called to check and to see how she was doing. I told him we just returned from the hospital. He asked if he could just come over and spend the night with the kids. He would sleep in the room with them. I said yes; he came over and stayed with them. Later that night I heard a loud noise; it was my jealous ex-boyfriend breaking into my house. I woke up with my kid's father lying next to me butt naked, holding me. That's all my ex needed to see; they started fighting while my kid's father was still naked. My daughter woke up, hollering, "Stop fighting my dad!" I was in between both of them, trying to break up the fight. When my ex-boyfriend started saying, "I know you were messing around with him. That's why you broke up with me." My kid's father was getting the best of him, but I always kept a metal pipe for protection in my house. He grabbed it and started hitting my kid's father in the head with it; then he heard the police siren. He ran outside and took the pipe and busted both of our windshields out. He got away from the police, and my sister pulled up. I called the ambulance for my kid's father. My sister followed us to the hospital. When we got there, my kid's grandmother and aunt were there, asking what happened. He was telling his mother that it wasn't my fault. I hadn't seen his mother and sister in four years; of course, his sister started telling me it's my fault. All he wanted to do was be with his family. Then she and my oldest sister were into it; my sister started telling her that the guy was really jealous and that's why I broke it off with him. And besides, he was dating a woman on his job. My kid's father received some stitches, then we went on our separate ways leaving the hospital.

Riding back home with my sister, she said, "I need to tell you something about your kid's father. He was always trying to hit on me." I asked her, "What do you mean?" She said, "He asked me to sleep with him." She seen I was upset and crying. I guess I wasn't hurting enough for her at the time. When I made it home and put my kids to bed, I received a call from my kid's father, saying he was going to have my door repaired. I told him the owner will repair the door. The detective just left, I pressed charges, they asked me for his information so they could contact him. We had to go downtown and place a personal protection order. He said he better be lucky that I didn't have my gun with me. I said, "I know you're mad at me. But can I ask you something? My sister said you propositioned her for sex." He started laughing, saying my sister dated several of his boys and he would never touch her. I hung up with him and immediately called my grandmother. My grandmother said she never believed that my kid's father would have tried to hit on my sister. She believed that it was made up. He came over to talk about what his mother did, and he was very sorry; he just wanted his family back. "People make mistakes, and you made some as well. You have to learn how to forgive." At this point what happened between him and my ex-boyfriend, he could never forgive me anyway.

Two months later his brother in law and I were at Super Kmart; we ran into the kid's brother-in-law. He asked why I didn't come to the wedding. I said, "Who got married?" He said, "Your kid's father just got married today." I knew he was still hurting, and I knew it was over at this point. After he got married, he never came over and checked on the kids. One day we saw him at the gas station. He was with his wife, and my youngest daughter said, "Mom, that's my daddy over there." So she yelled his name; he jumped in his car and pulled off and never said anything to us. I followed him home; and I told him, "If you ever see our children and don't speak, we will have a problem. You are taking this way too far." The wife and I had a couple of words; she was telling me her kid's father had nothing to do with her kids, he explained he wanted to keep the peace. That's why he didn't speak. I told him she had nothing to do with or say when it came to me and our kids. At the time he only lived three blocks from us. So I decided I needed to find somebody that's going to help me out 'cause I wasn't getting no support from him.

I ran into a guy I had known for years. His mother and my great-grandmother attended the same church. He always had a thing for making people laugh. He was a goofball at church. He was somebody I never thought I would never be attracted to. I thought he was a very nice guy; he was known to be a workaholic. He was working in the same plant my grandfather worked. God knows that was the worst mistake I ever made far as dating him. He started off very nice taking the kids to concerts, helping me with my nieces and nephews. I was just using him; I had no feelings for him. I knew my intentions were wrong, but never expected what was to come. He started talking loud to me in front of others, criticizing my weight and always trying to tear me down. He used to tell me, "I know you don't care for me. All you want is my money."

As time moved on, the abuse got worse. Abusing and tormenting me and my kids. It started off verbal, then it became physical. He started being very mean and disrespectful to my friends and family. Eventually, the abuse turned to my kids, hitting them and trying to discipline them. My self-esteem was so low. I was so depressed; my brothers weren't around to protect me. I ended up having a car accident, and he told me he was going to pay the bills and help me out 'cause I was off work. He started playing games, never helping me with bills, bringing other women to my house—anything to make me miserable. I told him I was pregnant so he could help with the bills. I was heavy at the time; you couldn't tell, "I wasn't". Then he started helping me pay the bills; he became more abusive. I told his mother what was going on, thinking she was a strong member of the church, I could talk to her and she would have enough sense to talk to her son about the abuse. She told me she was a deacon and had kids before she was married. Her husband helped her with her kids. "That's all my son is trying to do is help you raise and take care of your kids." I decided that I needed to get out of this relationship before one of us killed each other. He was starting to pick fights with my older nephew, his way of running my loved ones out of my life. So he could have me to himself and continue to abuse me.

After several years finally I left him; I wasn't able to return to work. I had lost my job due to the car accident. Nobody was financially helping me. I received an eviction notice had to move in thirty days. Nowhere to go, I didn't want to move in with family. I was embarrassed. How could I let this man treat me and my children the way he did? I ended up moving in with my girlfriend down the street. The same friend he was so nasty and mean to. I asked her to give me thirty days. I was receiving ADC at the time. I took that first check, and I went to the Katydid's Company, the kids and I started selling candy. I remember how much candy I sold for the church and how much money I earned, so I figured I could do it again. I needed to find my kids and I a new home. The gas station owner at store let us come and sell candy in front of his gas station.

The candy business was booming. We had to come up with a name to support us selling candy. People would ask us what's the cause. We called it the Boys and Girls Club. He was so jealous of how much money I made 'cause his cousins were selling candy and they would go back and tell him. He broke into my house before I moved in with my girlfriend; thank God, my kids weren't there. They had been through enough with him and me. Pouring ketchup all over my candy boxes and furniture. Neighbors called the police; to my surprise, one of the officers was my uncle (mother's brother). I was in the bathroom when the police arrived. My uncle kicked in the bathroom door because he thought the ketchup was blood, he thought I was hurt. The crazy fool was still sitting in the kitchen when they arrived. He started to fight with the officers because he was asked to leave. He said he wasn't going anywhere; he swung on my uncle's partner. My uncle told his partner I was his niece; they immediately handcuffed him and put him in the police car. I pressed charges, he was sentenced to some jail time, probation, and a PPO to stay away from me.

Throughout the summer, we made $20,000, I even hired little kids around the neighborhood to work. They earned money for school clothes. I found a house that I was going to buy, no more renting for us. I didn't have a job, so I went to my good older friend of mine who cosigned for us to get the house. From selling candy, I was able to put up the down payment. I had enough money left to pay the mortgage for six months. I moved into the house on September of 1993.

My brother was released from prison in November of 1993. One day I was riding down Joy Road. I thought I saw a guy that looked just like my brother. I pulled closer to see and to my surprise it was him. He came to live with me and started looking for jobs; do not ask me how, but my ex-boyfriend found me after he was released from jail. Telling me he wanted to help my brother get a job in the plant. He had met my brother in prison during a visit. I asked my ex how he found out where I stayed, all he said, was he wanted to make it right. I didn't want to be his friend. I didn't believe him. He always had negative energy. "How could you allow a man to treat you and your kids that way?" my brother asked, He looked at me and said, "I'm going to torture him, then his family to show him how it feels to hurt somebody." I sat my brother down and told him how depressed and miserable my kids and I were. I was gaining weight, missing my brothers being away from me, worrying about him while he was in prison and how he was being treated.

"While you were gone, a lot of things happened. I'm not making excuses of what I let happen, but I was at a low place in my life. I used him, and it backfired on me. I just wanted to see what I could get from him. Please don't do anything to him or his family. You will go back to prison and I can't take being away from you again. You promised me no more jail time. Your family needs you." I said, "Don't worry, he will get what's coming to him." I told him I was seeking counseling, and nobody would hurt me and my children again.

I went to talk to my great-grandmother about his mother whom she was friends with for years. She told me that lady believed in voodoo. It was a man that had a gambling problem and was married. He used to borrow money from her, then the man ended up leaving his wife. They never had any children together, but all of a sudden he was crazy about the lady. Then he got a divorce from his wife and married her. My great-grandmother told me the man thought he couldn't have kids; he ended up having three kids by her. Their first child was a girl, and she had a deformity of the hand. The second child was a boy; he was special, and the last one was a boy born with one testicle. My great-grandmother told me about people who believed in putting spells on you, making you do what they wanted you to do. I laughed in disbelief.

I talked to one of his mother's neighbors; she told me the same as my great-grandmother. Then she told me to run for my life. She said he was never right; his father used to beat him all the time. I'm not telling you this to make an excuse for my actions. I fell deep in depression; it's like I was drifting away and didn't like anything about myself. He became a tornado in my life and I never loved him. I really only ever loved one man in my life. It's nothing like your first love; the rest is just people you are fascinated with. I can't change what happened to my children and me. But I'm thankful to God that we didn't perish in this journey. He shielded us with grace and mercy.

He said, "Did you tell anyone what was going on?" I told him I was too depressed, so I stayed away from everyone. I talked to our

RELEASE

grandfather and asked if he could help get you a job. He asked "He said he going to put the referral in." I said, "Pray and believe. If you have faith, you will get in there." He told me he was so excited to see our other brother; he hadn't seen him in seven years. They had a very tight bond. He said, "I can't wait to hug him."

My brother was planning to be in town that next week. He just got home; we were planning to go over my older sister's house and have a family get-together. He was going to come over for a little while then go out with our cousins. He came over, hung out with the family, and was dressed to go out. When he left, my kids and I went to the movies. In the middle of the movie I started to get a migraine headache. When we made it home, the phone was ringing off the hook. When I got inside the house, I had twenty missed calls. Ten was from my brother in West Virginia, telling me that I needed to get to Henry Ford Hospital on West Grand Boulevard in Detroit. There was an accident involving our brother. Five missed calls from my grandmother. I felt something was wrong, so I went over to my older sister's house; we called my brother in West Virginia. He said they found my number and had him listed as a John Doe. I told my brother that I think our little brother is gone, after we went to the hospital. We got there; my whole family was there. I knew in my spirit something was wrong with my little brother. Especially when they asked us to come to the chapel. The pastor came in, explained it was a tragic accident; he was fatally shot in the head. He died on the scene. My grandmother started screaming and crying, "He just a baby". He was the same age as my daughter when she died, twenty-six!" I asked the nurse, "Can we see our brother, I worked in hospice so I know that we are allowed to see loved ones."

The nurse told us to let her prepare his body so we could see him. I immediately called my father and my brother to tell them that our brother was no longer here with us. My father said he was on his way down to the hospital. By the time he got there, we were in the room with my little brother. The rest of the family wanted to see him too; they only allowed them to come back to say goodbye. He had this look on his face I'd never forget. He had a look the look of shock, like, why? Like as if someone caught him off guard. As my father came into the room, blood started running through the bandage. I looked over at my father whom I haven't seen in years; he was devastated. I started crying, thinking about my other brother who didn't get a chance to say goodbye to him. Leaving the hospital, we were all devastated about our loss. I would rather for him to be in prison; at least we could see him again. I was thinking that he was right; he wasn't going back to prison. I called my brother, he broke down crying, telling me that he was trying to catch the next flight out. I told him to call me and let me know how much the ticket would cost. He called me back to tell me how much, when and what time he was coming in. I called my father, he said he would bury his son. Whatever my siblings and I decided, he would take care of it. I went down to the Department of Social Services because he had no life insurance for burial. My father paid the balance.

When my brother arrived, we decided to let him pick out our little brother suit. It was too hard for him to see him like that. People were offering us used suits to bury my brother in. I told my brother whatever he picked out I'll pay for it. It's the last gift I could give to him. I went over to my cousin's house to find out why they left him as a John Doe. To our surprise we found out it was a mistaken identity. My cousin had a mark on his head because he was fooling around with this married woman that worked at the bar. She and her husband were from Cuba. Two weeks prior my brother getting killed, my cousin was hanging out at the bar with this married woman, one of her husband's friends came in and saw her engaging in a conversation with my cousin. Her husband's friend came over and asked what she doing talking to this black man. He warned my cousin whose wife he was messing with. My cousin said to the guy he didn't care who her husband was. The guy threw his hands up, like, "I warned you." A good friend of the family who stayed in that neighborhood was at the bar that night. She told us everything that happened. That was her hangout spot. I received a call from my cousin's wife telling me the same story. She confirmed that he was having an affair with this woman. My cousin knew not to take my brother to a place where he had beef. The night my brother was murdered, he and my two cousins were in the back of the bar shooting pool when the Cuban woman's husband came into the bar. He grabbed her and said, "I heard you were messing around with this black man and being very disrespectful." He started hitting her with his fist and dragging her outside the bar and asking her where's the black man was she sleeping with you. My cousin went to the door to see what's going on; her husband asked him if he was the black man who was messing around with his wife. He said "No". My cousin asked my little brother to go outside to check on my cousin, when my brother came outside her husband fired a shot, hitting my brother in the head. He was dead at the scene. The ambulance came, to take her my brother and the Cuban's man wife to the hospital. The detectives came down to question her, but she was really terrified of her husband. She had made a statement about what happened, then they went out and picked her husband up.

When it was time to go to court, my whole family was there in the courtroom. My cousin was called as a witness. As he began to testify, the Cuban man started screaming innocent blood, "God, forgive me." They never could find his wife; she came up missing, so they didn't have a witness. He was only sentenced to two years in prison and deported because he had a gun, that didn't match the murder weapon. After my little brother's funeral, all the jobs started calling for him and I had to tell them he was no longer here.

Now my brother was getting ready to go back to home to West Virginia, my younger sister decided to move to Atlanta where her girlfriend lived. My oldest sister also left and moved to Bowling Green, Ohio. I never lived anywhere but Michigan; it's no place to run when you're hurting. That's how I felt; my memories of my brother were all through my new home where he resigned for a short time. I held on to his clothes and letters that he sent to me when he was in prison. When my siblings got settled in their new homes, I started missing them. Every chance I got, my children and I went visiting them. My older brother lived in a baby mansion off a lake and opened up a hair salon. It was successful. I was very proud of him. Losing our brother made us closer than ever. Years had gone by; it still felt like a knife cutting me. I learned to accept the fact that he was not coming back, every time we thought and talked about him, we were keeping his memory alive.

Three years had passed; my life was still broken. I wasn't interested in dating at all, till one day a friend of mind made me promise her; I would go see her son play football. It was so hot outside that day. I got off work and just wanted to lay up under some air. She came knocking on the door, begging for me to come on. I got dressed, and we went to the game. When we got there, we went straight to get something to drink from this ice cream truck. There was a man on the truck; he was a foreigner with a French accent. He asked me if I was married. I answered no. I wasn't interested in him at all, but he asked me why I came to a football game in all white. I never said a word. He started telling me that I was so beautiful and he loved my eyes. I said, "Thank you very much." We sat down, he got on the intercom and said he would give free ice cream and pop to anyone that could get the lady in the white shorts to give him my number. All the people at the game started saying that I should give him my number. He was a nice guy. So I ended up giving him my number. He kept saying thank you for giving him the opportunity to get to know me. He kept his word and gave everyone free ice cream and pop if they wanted it. I was impressed;

It was three weeks before I finally heard from him. It was a Friday night. I got a call; it was him asking me if I was free to go out tonight. He asked, "where could he pick me up from". I paused, thinking about all my bad relationships in the past. Then he said, "I want you to be able to trust me, you know where I work," I allowed him to come to my home. It was funny when he came to pick me up. He pulled up in his cab second job I'm assuming. My youngest daughter said, "Mom, did you call a cab?" I told her, "No, I didn't." Then it was a knock at the door. I peeped out; it was him with two dozen beautiful red roses and bottle of expensive champagne. I opened the door, he said, "Wow, I bought these for you." I said, "Thank you," he said, "Wow, you got a beautiful home. You sure you live alone with no man?" I told him, "Yes, I've been single for three years now." I introduced him to my kids; he asked me where their father was. I told him that their father lived three blocks from us

RELEASE

and was married. He had step kids, and we hadn't seen him in seven years. He said, "That's unbelievable how, a man can stay away from you and your kids." I asked him if he had any kids; he told me, "No, but I, do now. Your kids are very manner able." I told him thanks; we were getting ready to go, and I said we could take my car. He said, "No, we're taking my cab. You've got to get in the back because you are not allowed to sit up front." I looked at my kids, and they're cracking up, laughing. We left, and the night was wonderful; he was the perfect gentleman.

As time went on, he would always surprise me with gifts, taking me and my kids to see different things. It was always a pleasure being with him, and my kids enjoyed him too. He was a very busy man; a private school teacher, that was his profession. He had about four ice cream trucks and six cabs. He was supportive of exchange students that came from his country (Nigeria) by supplying them with room and board. He gave them jobs to support themselves and they paid him money for helping them while they were going to school. He slowly involved me in his business, trusting me to pick up money from all his places of business. He paid all my bills; it was nothing for him to give me two thousand dollars to buy my kids clothes and helping me with my siblings. A good family man he was! What a blessing!

One year on my birthday, I came home. I had a brand-new truck in my driveway with a bow on it. When he came over that evening, he had tickets for us to go to Miami. He told me that it was a big party there. He got us matching outfits customized from his country. They were so beautiful; he then picked out the shoes and my accessories; everything was already laid out for me. We left; we got engaged. He bought me a rare black diamond ring from his country, custom-made just for me. Telling me it's for me his queen. We made it to Florida; it was a surprise party for me. I was so happy. I had never been treated this good in my life. We stayed in a mansion; it was so gorgeous surrounded by blue waters. I can remember going to the party and people started bowing down to him, asking me, "Do you know exactly who he is?" And I said, "A schoolteacher." They laughed, telling me where he was from, and he was like royalty over in his country. His father was like a king in their village. He didn't want him to come to America; he was afraid he would come here and meet a woman get married and wouldn't come back to claim his inheritance. He wanted to show his father that he can make it on his own. I can recall a lot of people calling him from Nigeria asking him for money. He would always wire money home to help the poor. One day he came over and asked me to put a couple of his sports coats into the cleaners. I said I would, as I was checking the pockets, I found five thousand dollars in the inside of his pocket. I called him immediately and told him that he had left some money in one of his pockets. He started laughing, then he told me that I passed the test and to take the kids shopping I said, "Thank you."

Later on that night, he came over with a safe; he told me all the money that he collected he wanted to keep it here because he trusted me. He was ten years older than I, always thought he was teaching me something. I took him to meet my grandmother. She didn't take a liking to him at all. She said, "He isn't nothing but a drug dealer, and it was two ways out. Jail or hell." She said, "Why he wanted to meet me, so he can know where your loved ones at? I know he knows where your siblings stay." I said, "Yes, and he always gives me money to help them." She said, "I'm not impressed." "You already have a nice house and a good job. You always doing your own thing. You are already blessed." I just folded up a thousand dollars and put it in her purse, just smiling to myself. I always supported my grandmother to show her how much I appreciated, all she did for me and my siblings. He was promoting this singing artist from his country. He rented a hall, to throw a party. He asked me to rent three limos, one for the artist, one for me, and one for the kids to follow me. He took me and the kids to Somerset Mall. I saw this nice pair of shoes and purse, I asked the clerk how much they were because they didn't have a tag on them. He pulled me over to the side and said, "When you out with me, don't ever ask how much. If you have to ask how much it is, you can't afford it."

Leaving the mall on our way home to get ready for the concert, the limo Excalibur arrived an hour early, so we utilized the time riding around the city. My neighbors were taking pictures of us like we were stars. I felt like I was on cloud nine. That night I thought I was a queen. I was dressed in pearl linen and sequined, diamonds were everywhere. My engagement ring was something to talk about. We arrived. It was a packed house; he sold out. I had to call him and tell him we were outside. He came out and greeted us, when we walked into the hall; he had a table set up for us. He immediately took me to the dance floor to show me off; by this time I had learned how to do their native dance. The artist started to come over and dance with me, and he and my boyfriend started spraying me with twenty-dollar bills. When I was walking off the dance floor. This stranger grabbed my hand and started dancing with me while my boyfriend was at the door to check on his money. I was slightly intoxicated when the guy started dancing with me. I told him no because my boyfriend was highly jealous and the man started dancing around me, spraying me with more money. I was telling him, "Please stay away, I'm engaged," then he started following me all through the concert. When my boyfriend saw what he was doing he came up to me and said he needed for us to go home. He told me he would deal with him. I told him, "Okay," so my kids and I were getting ready to go home. He asked me to come get in his car and told me that I embarrassed him and our kids. I just knew to be quiet, then I told the kids to come in; we had the limo for two more hours. Before we left, he took a whole can of fruit juice and threw it on my beautiful dress. I still didn't say anything to him; I knew he started to think that he owned me. Like he made me what I am today. He said take this money that he collected home to put up; he would be by later so we could count to see how much we made. I still was silent with fruit juice all over me. I had to tell the limo driver to take me and the kids home. I ran into the house to take a shower, changing my clothes, to leave back out leaving the money at home. My kids and I went riding, so we rode down to Belle Isle and hung out, having a great night.

We returned; he was at home waiting on us. He was in the bed counting the money, telling me that he could have how many women he can afford. I still was silent. I started thinking that this relationship was about to end; he really started looking at me like I was personal property. He started belittling me, asking me where my

RELEASE

kids' father was and saying, "You weren't a virgin when I met you." I told him, "I never said I was." "Then the man that took your virginity, he is responsible for you."

I decided I was about to end this relationship. So I started saving, whenever he gave me some money, I put it up. For a punishment, he gave me three weeks off—no call, no show. I had the best three weeks ever. I partied. I had a ball. When he decided to come back around, this woman had followed him back to my house. I looked outside; she had blocked him in, telling me that she had been with him for twenty years and they were married with kids. He had four sons and he was never going to leave them. I explained to him that we needed to talk and discuss how this relationship was over and I wanted my keys back. He continuously stated we could talk when he got back and our relationship was not over. That was my confirmation it was time to leave this man. I started praying and asking God to release me from this situation without any harm or danger coming my way.

A couple of days following, he came over to the house, asking me for money, stating he was in a hurry to meet a friend. I was determined to go with him. We arrived at a hotel in Southfield, Michigan. We went up to the hotel room; the men were communicating in their language. He gave him the money; to his surprise, his friend gave him two games (Monopoly and Yahtzee) sealed as if he just left the store purchasing them. We were ready to leave the hotel, with the bag games inside. We proceeded to the cab. I explained to him that something didn't feel right, and six men were sitting in their cars alone. Once I explained this to him, he stated that I was paranoid. When we pulled off, these same six cars with the same men proceeded to follow us. Heading down Telegraph toward I-96 freeway. Once we reached Seven Mile and Telegraph, Redford police began to follow us as well. State troopers were behind in the six vehicles with the six men. We were pulled over at I-96 and Telegraph by the Redford police. He suggested that I hand him the bag so he could jump out and flee the scene. I refused to give to him the bags in fear of him being beaten or shot. He then told me what was inside of the games, and we could be sent away to serve natural life in prison. I began to pray and kept the bag with me still. He pulled the cab over

RELEASE

and jumped out and started running. Redford police told me they're taking me in for questioning. I was allowed one phone call. I called home, and my niece answered. I told her what happened and for her to call my attorney and then head to the police station. Being placed in a holding room, where there were a lot of bags on the floor where they also placed our bag mixed along with the rest. My niece made it to the station, and to my surprise, the officer gave her the bags and told her she could leave with them once their investigation was complete. She left then returned once the investigation was complete. She had the bags in the truck. FBI agents raided the truck and found the bags. The only good thing was it broke chain of evidence once she left. They were very upset with us so they bonded all three of us out. I was allowed to go to him because I was an American citizen. My boyfriend had his green card, so they let him go. The other guy didn't have his green card, so he had to stay in jail and they will let him go. When they took us down to get fingerprinted, the guy my boyfriend met at the hotel started threatening him, telling him that he never met me before and he was going to be telling the FBI everything. That he better wire his family fifty thousand dollars back home and he had forty-eight hours to do it. My boyfriend looked at me and told me not to pay attention. "Just keep looking at me with those beautiful eyes of yours. We will get through this." He told me, "I got you for life, trust in me."

When it came time for us to go back to court, I received a call telling me that the man that I and my boyfriend went to meet suddenly died while in lockup. My boyfriend came home wearing a tether; he started telling me that he was not going to let me go to prison. He said we got a good chance of the case being thrown out. At the beginning of the case we had the same lawyer, but now he had to find me a new lawyer. I went to meet my new lawyer; he was so nice, telling me that he was going to do the best he could to get me off. I told him, "I put it in God's hands. I've been praying to get out of this relationship, and my grandmother told me that it's only two ways out." I told him, "Just do your best." He told me that the Feds would be out to my house, and "Don't be afraid, it's part of the procedure." They didn't kick in the door, just started taking old pictures we had around my house. One of the agents said, "I just thought you were a passenger in the cab." I told him my name and if I could talk to my lawyer. Every question that was asked of me, I repeated it back to them. I knew they did that to get you to incriminate yourself, so I kept repeating the questions. "I would like to talk to my attorney."

It was time to go back to court to file a motion, or a motion to suppress hearing. The judge refused to throw it out now. We had to make a plea bargain or take it to trial. I decided to take it to trial; while I was awaiting my trial I started getting things in order because my oldest daughter was about to graduate from high school. I was thankful to God for letting me see her walk across the stage and go to prom. I was really happy that she was up in age so they couldn't put my kids in the system. A month before my trial began, FBI had dropped the charges on my boyfriend because they had no case against him. I came out of the hotel holding the bags. So the bag was mine unless I could tell them something different. I didn't know anything different.

One day he came over, telling me how grateful he was for me. He started telling me about some of his business associates talking, saying I knew too much; they told him not to trust me because if I went to trial and lose they thought I would be terrified and start running my mouth. They wanted to silence me; he was already going through problems back to him for what happened to the guy. I told him that I would die with what I know, and when I come home I was through with this life and this relationship.

I lost the trial, and I was sentenced to four and half years. Throughout the trial the prosecutor kept attacking my self-esteem about my weight problem and how men used obese women in the dope game. They were supposed to have my trial in Detroit, but at the last minute they changed my trial to Ann Arbor. It was one black person in the whole jury; the jury left and came back in one hour to tell me that I was guilty. My attorney came to the back to tell me that he was going to file an appeal on behalf of my case. Two detectives drove me over to Wayne County Jail; it was a holding center for the Feds. I woke up thinking it was a nightmare, but it was real. I called him, and everyone was in tears. I felt so bad; he told me that he was

RELEASE

sitting down with my attorney. The first attorney was known for representing big-time drug cases, so I told him no. The second one he sent, I just didn't have a good feeling about him, but the third attorney who came to see me was a short white man. He just got his license restored back in practice law; my case would have been his first case from the Supreme Court since he got his law license back. So I figured he would be the best for me. I prayed on my decision, then I called the attorney who represented me in my trial and told him that I was going with another attorney and asked if he had heard of him. He told me yes. I told him the reason why I chose him, I thanked him for representing me and setting up my appeal.

One day they called me and said I had a visitor, but it wasn't visitor's day. I went to see who it was; to my surprise, it was my father whom I haven't seen since my little brother's death. I walked right past him, and he called me by name. I turned around and said, "Dad." He said, "It's me." I sat down and started crying, saying, "I'm sorry." He said he never thought I would be in this type of situation. "I know I put a lot on y'all. But thank you for taking care of your siblings." He told me to tell everything I knew so I could come home to my family. I said I had four and a half years to go. I was appealing this case. He paid my attorney fees and took care of my kids".

When the visit was over, I called my grandmother to tell her about my visit; she said she had some bad news for me. That she had lung cancer; she was telling me that she would be okay, not to worry about her. She told me to stay around the older women while I was here; they would keep me safe and get involved in church. I was locked up with women that were hooked on heroine, vomiting and sick all night. I began taking care of them. God is good; he allowed me to see the damage that it caused to these women's lives.

It was time for me to transfer; they sent me to New Jersey, far away from my family. I wrote to the judge that sentenced me, I asked him if he could move me closer to home because my grandmother was very ill. The letters had to go to the prosecuting attorney and to my attorney. The judge wrote me back and transferred me to West Virginia. God is good all the time. I was able to see my kids. On their first visit they cried, upset with me for leaving them. I told them you

RELEASE

got to take the good with the bad. This was the bad; never involve yourself in this game. This was my out; my kids and him came down every other weekend. I could see it was very hard for my kids seeing me there, I asked him to send them on a trip, so he did.

Two months had passed before seeing them again. I began to lose weight, stressed out, waiting to hear an answer about my appeal. I had called home six times a day or more. My oldest daughter had my back all the way, taking care of her sister and checking on my grandmother, bringing her roses every day. I called my attorney; he told me that my hearing was coming up in the next week. I called my grandmother, she said she needed me to promise that I would never involve myself in this situation again. She told me that she was praying for me to be safe return home, and she was getting weak. She was giving up her ghost for me. My hearing was coming up in three days. I got a call to come to the office to hear the worst news that my grandmother had passed. The warden asked me if I wanted to go home shackled down and with an officer escort. The money wasn't the problem. I just didn't want to embarrass my family, so a close friend and her kids came down to visit me. We cried the whole visit. I went back to my room and wrote my kid's father, asking him to go by and check on the kids. He never did respond, I asked their godfather to move in with them to keep an eye on them while I was locked up. My baby girl started acting up, she was hurting because I was away. Lying in my room, crying my eyes out, my faith was strong.

My counselor came to my room and said, "Butler, you won your appeal. We got twenty-four hours to get you off the grounds." he said, "Follow me to my office, your attorney is on the phone." "We won, He said. This case changed the law. You shouldn't have been arrested." He told me to call home, I called home; they were all crying with joy that I was coming home. They asked me when I was coming home. I told them to take some money over to my girlfriend so she could charge me a flight home.

I arrived home around six that evening, greeted by my family and friends. I gave everything I bought in prison to this old lady who had a life sentence. She and I got baptized together; she always kept my spirits high when I was feeling low. God is good. I only had to do sixteen months of my sentence. I had been home for three months. I kept my promise not to be involved with him anymore. He came over to my house to give me some money and said thank you. He told me it's a guy at the hotel that wanted to hear my side of the story from his country because they didn't believe him. I drove to the hotel to pick him up, bringing him to the restaurant so we could talk. When we went to the hotel, the man was standing at the door waiting on me. I asked him if he knew my friend, then the FBI pointed their guns on me. I immediately was put in handcuffs and asked me where my friend was because they had the time taped listening to their conversation.

They took me to the station, I told them how he had tricked me to go to pick up this guy before the FBI picked him up. He fled the country. Since that day I never went back to jail like he wanted me to. I hadn't been in trouble in twenty years and never dated another man in the game.

One day I went to the doctor; they sent me for a mammogram. The test came back positive for breast cancer; I couldn't believe it. I went from doctor to doctor but same results. I said I take care of people, I was in denial. I finally decided to let go and let God handle it. The Holy Spirit was telling me he sent his boat, so aboard. I did just that—the treatment plan with surgery to remove the cancer. I took chemo to make sure it's all gone, and radiation treatment. All three treatments took one whole year. God is awesome; today I'm eleven-years' cancer-free. My children did an awesome job supporting me because I wasn't able to work, my brother made wigs for me and my sisters supported me to the end. I had so much love and support from my grandfather family and friends as well. God's grace and mercy never left me.

I had my share of challenges in life, but I made it. Through losing my mother and not having my father around, I made a way out of no way. Being only nine years of age when my mother passed; the worst experience ever. How was I supposed to grow and become a woman without her? How was I going to support my siblings as she asked of me? I was only nine. I was supposed to be enjoying life as a kid, having fun, getting into trouble, and playing with my friends.

RELEASE

I was robbed of my childhood. Instead I had to become a grown woman on my own and do what was best for me and my siblings. I know God does not make any mistakes. Yes, I've lost a lot, but God blessed me with positive gains. I made it financially possible to provide for my siblings as my mom wished, and we stayed together. I didn't have all the answers. I was still learning myself, but I promised my mother. I would do what she asked of me. Everyone is okay today and in good health, thank you, God. We lost our little brother, and we will never outlive that day. Despite his choices, I'm glad we gave him someone to look up to, he respected me as such.

I can only hope my mom is proud of me. I have two beautiful children and four grandchildren that are the love of my life. I was even blessed with a grandson, and he was born on my mother's birthday, such a beautiful gift. I have learned to protect them with every part of me. I just wish my mother could have met her grandchildren and made memories of her own. She would have loved them as I do. She would have enjoyed all of her great-grandchildren. I hate that we were robbed of her. I have to remember that God makes no mistakes my journey was necessary. I have a testimony and I'm a living witness of the goodness of God. For I have been tried and tested. Mom, I hope you are proud of the strong woman I've become. I made a lot of terrible decisions, not only did I put myself through hurt and pain, but my children as well. Thank God, they love me wholeheartedly and was able to forgive me. I know it wasn't easy and my choices have affected their lives in many ways. All I can hope is, they have learned from my mistakes. Yet, throughout it all, I survived, we survived. We are never too old to learn a better way. We don't know what situations we will be put in or the choices we will make; we are only human. I just have to be grateful that I am still here today. 2Timothy 4:7, "I have fought the good fight, I have finished the race, I have to keep the faith." Moving forward is the key; everyone has a story, and I'm honored to share mine. Thank you, God.

About the Author

At the age of nine, she took on the responsibility of helping in raising her siblings after her mother passed. She became a mother at the age of nineteen; she was in special education until she managed to get her GED. She became a certified hospice home health aide and coordinator. She was a single parent raising two kids on her own. But at the age of forty-six, she was diagnosed with breast cancer. Thank God, she is in remission. In 1999, she went to federal prison, which was the worst day of her life. In May 2010, she received the highest award in health care, the Sherman award. One time in her life she was 340 pounds; successfully she lost 140 pounds. When she went to the hospital to have surgery, a jealous guy she was dating tried to kill her while in recovery at St. Johns in Macomb, Michigan. When she awakened, she was told that she had slipped into a coma and had to have a blood transfusion due to her blood loss. When she was release from hospital, he started calling her, making threats of what he was going to do to her. He got in a tragic accident on the freeway awhile after this incident while he was driving, his daughter stated to me. She said his body was ejected through the windshield; he was in a coma for three days and passed away. On the other hand, she is now retired from two back surgeries still walking around and had two car accidents. Thank you, God that she is still here. Having faith is everything.